The Sadness I Take to Sea
and Other Poems

The Sadness I Take to Sea
and Other Poems

MICHAEL THOMAS BRIMBAU

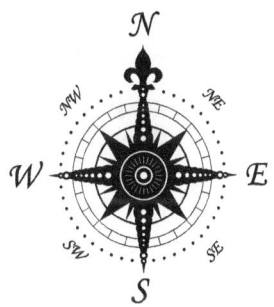

PEARTREE PRESS: FALL RIVER, MASSACHUSETTS
2014

PearTree Press
P.O. Box 9585
Fall River, MA 02720
peartree-press.com

All rights reserved. No part of this book may be used or reproduced in any manner whatsoever scanned, or distributed in any printed or electronic form without written permission from the publisher, except in the case of brief quotations embodied in critical articles and reviews.

For information, write us at PearTree Press, P.O. Box 9585, Fall River, MA 02720.

Library of Congress Control Number: 2014941844

ISBN-10: 0-9819043-8-6
ISBN-13: 978-0-9819043-8-2

Printed in the United States of America on acid-free paper.

Book design by Stefani Koorey
Photography by Stefani Koorey and Michael Thomas Brimbau

Copyright © 2014 by Michael Thomas Brimbau

Printed in the United States of America

1 3 5 7 9 10 8 6 4 2

for Donald Winland
teacher, confidant, friend

Introduction

Some of the poems written here were done so over thirty-five years ago. Many are simplistic in their harmonic metre and somewhat juvenile and unsophisticated in both substance and verse, while still others are green and unseasoned in their approach to life, relationships, and the world in general. Many were meant to be lyrical, written to song.

On the coast of Southeastern Massachusetts is a little spit of land called Horseneck Beach State Reservation. Horseneck, as the place is commonly known to locals, is located in the tranquil town of Westport and overlooks Buzzards Bay, the Elizabeth Islands, and Rhode Island Sound. The north side of Horseneck is a maze of grassy marshland—the south, an endless sandy beach stretching for over two miles.

The area has secreted potent inspiration for many of the poems here. As a young man, I had spent a great deal of time wandering Horseneck Beach's golden, sandy dunes, hiking the lumpy landscape of Gooseberry Island, or shuffling along the pimpled, rocky shore of East Beach. I would lay myself down on a smooth sandpaper shore, under an unyielding sun, and listen to the placid melody of a plowing surf, or walk late past midnight, and into the early morning hour, along a burnished stony beach, where I would make love to the sea, the moon, stars, and sweetheart.

An alliance between sky, salt, and pubescent love took birth on the beaches of Horseneck. It has been a harbor of joyful tranquility and somber repose—and at times, an accommodation for sadness and melancholy. A place of weeping pain—of boundless retreat, one which at times inflamed and muffled death—the loss of a younger brother, the passing of a loving mother, and even the demise of Shannon and Henty, my beloved tail-wagging companions. Horseneck is a special place of contrasting emotions, which pampers the heart, cleanses the mind, and inflates the soul—a hospice for one's poetic psyche. Though few of the poems here were ever completed there, a good portion of them had their dawning at Horseneck.

Michael Thomas Brimbau

CONTENTS

The Sadness I Take to Sea

Sakonnet Shore	3
Fat Moon	4
Newport Gleam	5
In This Cuttyhunk Storm	6
Reading the Waves	8
Threading Needles	9
The Sadness I Take to Sea	10
Rowing	11
From Wave to Wave to Wave	12
What a Rush That Was	15
The Fog Surreal	16
High and Dry	17
What God Has Placed Around Them	18
How Many Can There Be	20
I Was Alone	22
Leaving No Prints	24
By These Hidden Stones	26
Upon Martha's Throne	28
To Another Face	29
If Not for This Ocean	30
To A Swimming Dock	31
And Not Conform	32
Forgot My Key	33
At Jackie's Beach	34
New England Clouds	36
And the Waves All Bow Away	38
Good Bye Teddy Boy	39
On This Cuttyhunk With You	40
Toast for Breakfast	42

My Stefani

Your Orlando Beach	46
Napkin Poem	48
Furnace	49
The Wind in Our Song	50
Spooning With You	51
Florida Sun in My New England Sky	52
Your Love Came to Pass	53

Unable to Quench	54
Autumn Nest	55
By This Open Bedroom Door	56
My Stefani	58
Kiss Me Sweet Laddie	60
Turnovers and Kisses	62

The Enemy's Love

Horseneck	66
Knowing You	68
A Daisy	69
Zooming Turtles Born Free	70
Another Monday Morning (song)	73
Painting Dreams (song)	74
November Search (song)	76
Autumn of My Eye (song)	78
The Struggle	80
The Enemies Love (song)	82
Skunk's Tail	84
Brenda's Eyes (song)	86

Watching the Monkey

My Stranger, My Lover	90
I End My Day	93
Cardoza	94
Blind Date	96
Twelve Over Twelve	98
Ardith in the Rain	99
Sell Me ... Adore	100
By Bread ... Alone	102
Down the Aisles of Oak Grove	103
Watching the Monkeys	104
I Be Your Butter Your Jam	107
Thru the Mall	108
Need Ask God, What For	111
Your Weakness Does Mar	112
Sacred Anvil	114
Friendship Passes Away	116
Where I Can Never Go	118

The Darkness

Poetry Is	123
Waiting	124
Ice House at Interlachen	125
Borden Utopia Gone	126
Upon Filming Interlachen	128
The Pawn	130
The Darkness	132
Void in the Earth	134
Depression Train	136
To Australia	138
Met a Man	139
You are Aging Gracefully	140
Rainbow Clown	141
Animals Animals	142

The Sadness I Take to Sea

Sakonnet Shore

My tiny ship floats
     on the whisper
     a breeze
delivered from the cloudless sky
     where the orange moon
     sizzles from the watery east
in this kissable night
upon a crimson horizon
where distant birds
skim the waves
and a lighthouse winks
     teasing me with delight
     standing on a Sakonnet shore
like a friendly Cyclops
illuminating a silver sea.

Fat Moon

The fat moon rises to
      salute the crisp of night,
my anchor and thin line
      hold my ship
like a pup on a leash—
      she wanders all about
twisting in the evening wisp,
      she sways me in slumber
          upon the twinkling of wavelets
flopping and plopping
it sings me to sleep
under the warm night summer wind
and black diamond speckled sky.

Newport Gleam

In this Newport gleam
        my vessel looks upon the golden land
the barren cooling sand
        where faceless masses once lounged
on elfin wood, cotton strip chairs
        with umbrellas never to kiss the rain
with towels for rugs
        to guard from the biting sand
in the warmth of day
        as restless children play
in the wet folding summer surf
        now vacant to the cool night breeze
that blows softly out to me.

        and the waltz of this lonely hull
off this horseshoe Newport shore
        skates along a wrinkled bay
caressing the playful waters of Third Beach
        that cradles a desolate night
in the hollow darkness all around.

In This Cuttyhunk Storm

The steel strings of my rigging
   quiver with the sound of a fife n'
flute
      above the trembling waters
         kissing sailors with fear.

this tiny bobbing vessel warps to the
   twisted nylon cord which
      creaks this umbilical
         in the darkness n' roar.

I crawl these salted decks
   a mate pickled by pelting rain
      afraid of the sunken wrecks
         in the gale of the main
chilling a seaman's chest
clutching the wheel
like a turnbuckle heart
of cold brass and steel.

Pease and Whale rocks
   beckon to me
      to beach the keel
         without making a plea
upon a grassy sand spit
by the lee of the storm
to scuttle the days
marooned and forlorn.

my vessel it sings
   to the squall that rings
      the headland buoys
         past wire and mast
with violin halyards
scream songs from the past
that howl and bellow
to the anchor I cast.

I'm below at last
   from the chaos above
      to watch the night pass
         on this ship which I love.

and when all is said and done
I would not choose
or exchange for a berth
or wish to be torn
to the safety of shore
      in this Cuttyhunk storm.

Reading the Waves

Sailing along
curious waves
with the whites of
their eyes, crying
        forth wet.

breaking with
        simmer in tumble
they peek over
        Your shoulder
at the words
        held far from land
as You sit at watch
with binding in hand.

turning damp pages
        You do so slowly
like a virtuous choir girl
        with hymn book
and spray
        in Your ocean pew
with the preaching sea
blowing aft and away
as the foamy swells grew.

For SK, reading her book 100 miles off Cape Hatteras.

Threading Needles

We thread needles
        heaving, boiling,
a caldron of sweeping swells
with ireful lions
riding their shoulders
leaping as the slogging claws
dissolve into turquoise halos
              beside You.

it was an angry sea
charging, but not at us,
nothing personal you see.

we were two prowlers
snaking boldly along
pretending to be lion tamers
in a watery world that perhaps
we should not be,
sewing the waves
one to another
intruders
threading needles
              in an endless sea.

The Sadness I Take to Sea

The mouth of this river
in a salty saliva of foam
spits me out

      I sail alone,
my tiny ship
chops through this stormy swell
just outside the bay
as the sun hides from me
its solace, its warmth,
      as You hide from me
      your desire to be free

and the gale, this spray
is a struggle I will wage
a welcome escape
with a rival enraged

      and in the same breath
      while keeping me wet
      it comforts me

and more distant the shore
the more the horizon calls to me
and the sadness left upon land
is the sadness I take to sea

and before this ship I turn
I pray that you may burn
passion once more for me.

Rowing

We row this bucking dingy
into a sloppy, angry chop,

suddenly—
a rouge, icy wave slaps
and splashes down the small
of my back,

—it sends a chill up my spine.

You cup your hand to Your mouth
and laugh at the queer look I display,

careful not to tip this tiny vessel
You kneel before me,

—I stop rowing.

Your hands resting on my knees
You brace Yourself
lean in
and place Your warm lips
softly on my needy, red cheek,

Your lashes tickle my nose
Your hair brushes my brow

I close my eyes.
suddenly—
it's dead calm
and, it sends a chill up my spine.

                                For SK

From Wave to Wave to Wave

And,
from wave to wave to wave
        to sea
You said you'd chase and sail
        with me
to a distant space we'd get away
and in my life you said you'd stay
        where new horizons
           will set us free.

who is to know
or can maintain
a spark of pleasure
a measure of pain,
        only time can speak
or make plain.

so,
over swell and swell and swell
        this ocean
to pursue our dream to enhance
        the notion
as the sun slips slowly across the sky
with love at the helm
        our desire will try
           to keep this craft in motion.

And,
from wave to wave to wave
        to sea
You said you'd chase and sail
        with me
to a distant space we'd get away
and in my life you said you'd stay
        where new horizons
           will set us free.

who is to know
or can maintain
a spark of pleasure
a measure of pain,
        only time can speak
or make plain.

so,
over swell and swell and swell
        this ocean
to pursue our dream to enhance
        the notion
as the sun slips slowly across the sky
with love at the helm
        our desire will try
           to keep this craft in motion.

and with our bond
and a little cold rain
no storms to ride
or gales to tame
        we'll sail by the lee
from which we came.

and,
from wave to wave to wave
        to sea
you said you'd chase and sail
        with me.

though the clouds may hide the sun
in a following breeze
this boat will run
the way we should
or meant to be.

What a Rush That Was

I was sailing along
under full sail
trying to outrun
a cold front that was chasing
me down, under the Mount Hope Bridge

but up I had, too much sail
before I knew it
a puff buried the rail
I was not sure
if I should steer
or I should bail

after cutting a line
stiff and hard
as a steel rod
leading to a sail sheet
my vessel rose up
back up to its feet

what a rush that was,

not much different
from the first time
I saw you

I fell over in a puff of ardor
only later to have to bail
cut the line
get to my feet
and away to sail

what a rush that was.

The Fog Surreal

The distant shore blurs and fades
as the clotting fog unfolds,
a muffled damp blanket
in visions that refuse to focus
        like sleep without slumber
        a world within a world
        awe within wonder
        to drift within a pearl

the hollow silence roars
a vacuum of deafness
to sail into a cloud
tranquility without error
        fractured by a lonely horn
        upon the shore
        a distant warning
        sounding up this soupy bay
        a reminder that life is at hand
with death never far away.

High and Dry

The keel bumps the sea floor
the rigging shudders
and the waves slap
the hull in playful disregard
to blunders embraced
as we do lie
by the lee of the land
high and dry.

we will sit the gunwales
watch the sun as it slumps
in orange embarrassment
waning against a cloudy horizon
leaving us to wait the sea
with a new dawn tide
to set this vessel free.

till then we will lurk
these decks and bump
watch the laughing ducks
circle and beg
as we shudder and sway
with the evening breeze
in sleepless darkness
where we will lie
by the lee and by land
high and dry.

What God Has Placed Around Them

I sit the drizzled deck of this sloop
raw dampness permeates, seeping
my clothing and soul weeping
an icy repose fixed and alone
as I would want it
no other way

the late night breeze fans the musk
of stale seaweed, salt, and dry rot
decay from these gray splinted docks
like the ripened bones supporting the
spongy flesh
refusing to move
and go below
tuck into an arid bunk

stillness burrows its way
to my sleepless inebriated mind
a numbness, I belong here
the calm water is all around
a black mirror
where a solitary jellyfish pumps and wanders
the inky bottom by the swaying moss and grass
that sheet, the stones
a leafy bed for a starfish
a poising, prickly, burnt orange orb.

the moon has gone to India
to wed the sun
a bridge arched across the bay
with its necklace of light stretches
the misty night horizon
with its road to nowhere
and feeble mindless bastards
with no time
with no thought
to what God has placed around them.

How Many Can There Be

I sit by my anchor
and watch out to sea
and keep asking myself
how many can there be,

of drops in this ocean
of water all around
the number must be great
the quantity must astound,

and I look to the shore
to a long stretching beach
to the shoals that lie there
how far does it reach
        for each grain of sand
        that slopes to the sea
        I keep asking myself
        how many can there be,

and this night shroud above
stars fill the sky
pinpricks so bright
a feast for the eye
how many can there be
I could count till I die,

and these questions I ask
in my own desperate plea
to give meaning to life
to give meaning to me
and on this boat I count
how many can there be
just one lonely soul
afloat in the sea.

I Was Alone

I was alone—
        I didn't know it
placed newborn
in a small iron manger
where I lay solo, roaring
in the nip open air
where I felt one heart only, beating.

I was alone—
        I didn't know it
riding a Boston elevator
in a sky-rasping building
in a soaring box of musty crackers
toiling amongst the swarm
like a grape off the vine
before it was wine.

I was alone—
        I didn't know it
when I met you,
when I loved you,
when I held you,
in a vacant bed
which became crowded by thoughts
of other lovers, imposing,
embezzling the vacant night.

I was alone—
       I knew it
battering ocean swells
more miles offshore
than my age could count
ascending and plunging
through a fizz of laughing waves
where I long to stay
solo,
to kiss the cold desolate spray
praying that ultimately
I was alone.

Leaving No Prints

You walk the beach
along the fizz and surf
as foam and bubbles
tickle our feet
with the water they meet
      the ever-thirsty sand
      sucking at our toes
with swallowing kisses.

You walked ahead
I follow
ambush amblers
prowl behind us,

with every footprint
You leave
I insert mine,
      a small comfy sandal
      obscuring your impression
      concealing You
from the surf of others
that surround us,
slurping You in
with their eyes
as You stroll unaware.

      though they think
      they see You,
      You are
      just an apparition
      a seraph
leaving no footprint
in the sand ahead
where I am led
behind you.

By These Hidden Stones

I sail this forsaken water
        this New England shore
with rocks all around
not quite sure
how I arrived
in escaping the blow
how I will head
this harbor this foe.

in that respect it mirrors
my existence ashore
among the stony crowd.

I drift these shallow waters
escape the fleshy green reef
unlike the ones in my canvas
that cause me no grief.

and not unlike the wandering
I do on the shore
the challenge is hidden
beneath the draft that I draw.

still the trial I've been given
along this bouldery beach
is one I have chosen
one that will teach.

without a chart or first mate
I have a wish to escape
lay by this rock water
accepting my faith,

and on this summer bay
I need just anchor
study and wait,

and bearing I will find
not really afraid
of being ambushed,
with little fear
of the hordes ashore
and a waterless tear
to await a friendly tide,
and until then
be safer here.

Upon Martha's Throne

My vessel sways to the morning ebb
in a breakwater shroud
behind a bracelet of stone
in a small Vineyard cove
upon Martha's throne.

the limp dampened main
hangs from the boom
to this mooring I came
a morning in June
sailed through the rain
to this tiny lagoon.

on a sea haven spit
a violin he does play
a minstrel in training
in the birth of the day
in black tux and tails
a one-man cabaret.

his bow he swings
to a classical note
to the seagulls above
to me, to my boat
    a cadence in love
    as I drift, as I float
    in a Vineyard cove
    the music he wrote
upon Martha's throne
and a tear in my throat.

To Another Face

This peaceful bay
speaks to me
where I drop anchor
from the waters above
to the floor of the sea

but, it creeps and it drags
not digging in
        and I find it a sin
        that I must withdraw
to another place

unlike the anchor
you dropped
into my essence
where its rusty flukes
have dug deep.

wherever you go
I drag along
into stormy waters
        where the swell does heave
        where I find it a sin
        that I can't leave
to another face.

If Not For This Ocean

If not for this ocean
where would it have come
the waves and the motion
and the hunger undone
when I search for emotion
it's to you I have come
your love and devotion
to you I will run.

if not for this desire
in this billow which I sail
keel plows ever higher
in this tempest, in this gale
I'll keep warm, the fire
for you I'll not fail
with resolve I'll not tire
this sea I will scale.

and if not for the passion
I carry as crew
adoration comes crash'n
as you and I knew
this love we must ration
a love that is true
till this ocean I'll fashion
a route home to you.

To a Swimming Dock

You swam to the navel of the lake
and your heat there you did take
to a swimming dock
moored in the open water
a commune of bathers
where I cannot go.

you sit to simmer in the sun
your chin on your knees
till your anger is done,
and since I cannot swim
I'm left with my infraction
to deal with abandoned discord
as pale-back boys swim
and dive around you.

on this beach made of stone
I'm left forlorn to atone
if these pebbles be diamonds or gold
I would gladly exchange
a place upon that pine island float
or trade for an oar and tiny boat
to take me to you.

And Not Conform

On a beach full of rounded stone
in battering wave of social demand
tumbling with the surf I'm thrown
to these sculptures embedded in sand,

and these granite eggs, unmoving
with conformity they refuse to shift
orthodoxy the crutch they are proving
that set those of indifference adrift,

and my edges are rough and chipping
life has not been simple on me
they care not that their being is slipping
while I set my convictions all free,

but in a world of unyielding norms
molded by the swarms around
with the apathy this commune scorns
those who dare dig up this ground,

and this beach of marbles, rounded
I will scrape and carve a path
without freedoms and colors unfounded
to lie down and lay flat,

when the conformist waves flow over
to shape them all alike
I will tumble, roam and turnover
and kick, struggle, and fight
and not conform.

Forgot My Key

My outcast vessel
pivots above the river floor
from afar she calls out for me.

but,

I am stranded upon this dinghy dock
for at home I left the key
to unfasten my pram
take me from where I am
to my sloop and out to sea.

At Jackie's Beach

We sit on pastelly beach chairs
as the surf flows around
we sink ever deeper
the waves grow steeper
        and your heart
           begins to pound.

I clutch your hand
you look over— you smile
knowing all the while
that I understood
        while we sit amongst the flow
        I would never let go
of this love we began.

you softly close your eyes
throw back your head
your cheeks blushy red
        in the hot summer sun
        we sit sipping cheery rum
in this wet sand bed.

hot noon wind flows your hair
across your mouth, your face
in this magical sandy place
        I lean in and kiss your cheek
        you pretend not to peek
        from under your brimmy hat
and continue to smile
feeling no denial
I will continue to speak
of my love for you.

                                                          For Jackie 2006

New England Clouds (song)

New England clouds
are very low
they hide the sky
of blue,
and though the sun
came out today
I still keep
missing you.

and the waters of
Old Horseneck
are dyed a
gloomy gray
at the sands where
we first loved
thick clouds get in the way.

when you said you'd be going
I vowed I would not come
when love's no longer flowing
hearts no longer drum

and on the drawn horizon
my mind it cannot find
or wrap my thoughts around you
find a place to cast my line.

a hand of sand
I toss to sea
to wish the ache away,
where seabirds soar
apart from me
and a gale my heart can't slay.

New England clouds
are very low
they hid the sky
of blue,
and though the sun
came out today
I still keep missing you
I still keep missing you.

As the Waves All Bow Away

I wore this lonely vessel
by the breakwater and the bay
though winds were sometimes heavy
still, I had a pleasant stay

but now I start my journey
in the late hour of my day
with the harbor slowly fading
as the waves all bow away

and the swells, the swells they carry
my soul with God to stay
and this sea strips me of worry
to steam on through the spray

now my soul is sailing softly
far from where my body lay
with my Maker at the tiller
these breakers all obey
and I no longer need a pilot
as the waves all bow away.

*For William Schley-Ulrich,
September 27, 2009*

Good Bye Teddy Boy

On the sea you now take
may your compass be true
where your heart will not ache
and dreams you can now woo.

good-bye Teddy boy
may our course one day pass
where our vessels may cross
and our passions we'll cast.

good-bye Teddy boy
now your sails are all down
and your anchor is out
to the peace you have found.

good-bye Teddy boy
from a sailor in pain
the loss of a sea lion
in our hearts you remain
good-bye Teddy boy
good-bye.

Upon the death of Teddy Kennedy

On This Cuttyhunk With You

We climb all afternoon
so we can command a view
of the cliffs and the sea
where the eagles all flew
    where I wanted to be
        on this Cuttyhunk with you.

and in the distant horizon
where the rollers all live
tiny ships sail by
with all life has to give
under a lucid blue sky
    I would not want to live
    without you close by.

you point in the direction of home
towards the Westport beach
and laugh at how far
from home we have reached
    the distance to a star
    I'm left without speech
    as you kiss my lips
you always did teach
that you loved me.

as you look to the heavens
I brush your hair aside
you cuddle me with kisses
with your lips you divide

I embrace you in bliss
from you I won't hide
and Cuttyhunk I would miss
without you by my side.

Toast for Breakfast

Indifferent beggars
small floating cadets
a navy of mallards
circle the sloop
      a feathered procession
      in this sheltered cove
where we float
sounding for their morning meal

you feed them bread
and I am certain
on this quiescent stony coast
      when we are ready
      breakfast will be served
and with honks
and quacks
we will offer them our scraps
on a magic Cuttyhunk morning.

My Stefani

Your Orlando Beach

On this Orlando beach
I bask in Your glow
radiating from
      Your fingers
      Your skin
from your heart within
blazing inside mine
on this silk dune beach
we lay
where I choose my soul
    with my Love to stay.

shut my eyes
delight in the rolling swell
      Your voyaging hands
          sailing fingers
            sultry touch
caressing my desire
    by Your warmth
         Your fire
to laze here with You
thaw with the night
our love we renew
as You pout out the light.

with tender cool breeze
upon my bare back
made warm by lips
fiery but gentle and
wet as the salty sea
by tears of bliss
that fall upon me
on Your Orlando beach
      where I long to be.

Napkin Poem

I sit at this rocky table
      by the window of this
           empty café,
outside staring
my time bearing—
      without You.

the street—
grey rain paints by day
this window to the world
as people pass unaware
I think and I stare—
      about You.

the waitress pours me
      a smile
a fresh cup to drink
I focus on You once more
to the love You have in store
      where my dreams
      want to stay
      by this little café.

Furnace

The love
nuggets You give
and lay at my feet
white pearl love
I can never deplete
        feeding my fire
        stirring my hope
        igniting desire
        help me to cope,
and like
a red glowing furnace
I accept Your kind gift
and glow free with joy
the spirit You lift.

        to keep yourself warm
        all You need do
        is stand close by me
        this fire's for You
and will continue to burn
Your sorrows I'll drain
the fire You built
will not be in vain.

The Wind in Our Song

The hot winds of Florida
at times tepid and warm
are neither as fierce
never as strong
as my arms around You
where we know you belong
for the heat we emit
is the wind in our song.

Spooning With You

In a forlorn fetal poise
I lay in repose

like twins
in a cotton womb
in solace and comfort
You tuck your firm bony knees
carefully behind mine,

You rest your head on my shoulder
Your cheek on my neck
wadding breasts to my back
a spongy cookie tin
for my sorrow,

one arm creeps under my waist
the other on my cheek
Your hand comes to rest
            on my heart—

You are always
behind me
when I need You.

Florida Sun in My New England Eye

The falling snow
this icy stream
plummet and flow
through my very being

and these ancient trees
that soar and lean
in this Westport wood
by pine shrub and green

scratch at the clouds
on this frosty crisp day
melting slate snow
where I make my way

and these primeval walls
by which I like roam
divide field and wood
with timber from stone

and as the bitter wind
blows limb and pine
I miss Your heart
your cheek upon mine

and my thoughts of you
I cannot deny
the Florida sun
in my New England sky.

Your Love Came to Pass

You sit with me
earth by country
where I can count
sunrises over hay, but the wood
where time rests still
passing years that are good,
        on a honeysuckle-laced wall
        seated by an empty pasture
        marigolds, daisies, jade tall grass
        bullion silk hair,
                crimson thaw lips,
                Your love came to pass.

Unable to Quench

The faint martini light
gleams from above
upon cold lonely hands
      only the hot coffee in
      this steamy cup
      warms these fingers
left icy and wanting
of Your caress.

infant lovers share the next booth
their yearning bodies, adoring bookends
press hard at the edge of the table
      with drink
unable to quench their thirst
face to face
in moronic stare
reminding me.

I sip from this cup
with lips left tingling
like last we kissed
sweltering in distant embrace
      my nose, my mouth
lodged in Your fiery, fleecy neck
lonely fingers made warm
caressing Your back
as I cuddle this
scorching cup
press hard at the edge of the table
making love in reverie
unable to quench.

Autumn Nest

I can provide only
his rickety Autumn nest
a lofty sieve
where I give birth and cache
liquid dreams, fancies
to hatch—beg alone
in the cold open breeze.

You declare You need little more
more than a floating manger,
that relationships based
on fragility can root
in muddy soil
and in your mind
You have made concessions
for the sweeping snows
knowing full well
that summer will return.

chirp You will
that You are primed
to bear detriment in flight
weave Your own twigs
to live with crow
amongst unhatched aging eggs
to sway in my autumn nest
and watch the naked world
                        go by.

By This Open Bedroom Door

I lay here face down
wrinkled, pressed
pillow cold and dank
desert sheets dry
      departed wanting
      dry of You.

a soft chilly breeze
chews at my feet, my toes
up to my back and the small
by a door left open
when You embezzled
the warmth of embrace
away
far with You.

these paper sheets
this unsheltered bed
will be my ice pan
a cold sane asylum
where I will hide
on a tundra of cotton gloom
till You return
to close the door once again
bring back moist lips
the mist of love

to warm this frozen river bed
make wet this tide
put fast this flow
that awaits and slumbers
till You come again—
open this bedroom door.

My Stefani

Set adrift
        in sunset of life
I ponder the blunders
        I have made,
to miss a heart and lose at love
while tepid wind nips and fades,

and as I watch
        the sun go down
beyond the trees
        across the sea
of life I have forestalled
to watch my dreams
        slip apart from me.

And as my ship sails
        far in time
it's late to alter
        the long years right
all my hope will not sail back
upwind in the fading light,

from the east
        down to the west
I let in haste
        ambition fly
in my crossing I've done my best
still a tear drops from an eye

then when I felt
        all was lost
the sun turns back
        to rise again
west to east it starts to climb
        from where it was
        to where it's been.

and there you are
        to my disbelief
I hear you say:
        "please come to me"
and when it appeared the ship was lost
God sent you here—my Stefani.

Kiss Me Sweet Laddie

Kiss me sweet Laddie
though your tongue cannot speak
if I have done what is right
why must dusk air so bleak

'tis three weeks dawn summer
I clench onto life
endowed me by father
but not by his wife

and, when the jay starts to caw
the bee governs her hive
with cup tulips a bloom
warm breezes arrive

from the trials of August
buds forth maples in June
birth springs so young
my soul parts so soon

I yearn my ain country
this hull lists as I sail
Royal Nelson at helm
Donald Stuart at bail

tell me sweet Laddie
will I meet spring no more
give me sweet kisses
time of year I adore

and as the advent of Summer
strikes brazen and bold
will it leave me in darkness
has my poor soul been sold

kiss me sweet Laddie
though you can't hold my hand
life slips through so swiftly
as a screen filled with sand

I'm alone dear Father
Emma where can you be
kiss me sweet Laddie
I'm afraid can't you see
      kiss me sweet Laddie
      light fades
      comfort me
      kiss me sweet Laddie
kiss me
kiss me
(whisper) kiss me.

                                        Upon the dying of Miss Lizzie Borden
                                        with her Boston Bull Terrier, Laddie.

Turnovers and Kisses

I live for turnovers and kisses
it's what I desire
a stroke from your fingers
for I will not tire,
the apples you offer
puffed pastry n'sweet
with ruffles of passion
from your lips to my feet.

I live for turnovers and huggies
winding legs and arms
to swallow my torso
with beauty unarmed
to saccharine my tea
your infuser, your charm,

layered flaky love
dripping with fruit
caress so fragrant
my soul you recruit
in weakness I somber
spent with delight
no frosting or want
for care, or to fight.

I live for turnovers and kisses
to start off my day
and discharge all my profits
in your hand where I sleigh
and melt within light
in adoring foray,

I live for turnovers and kisses.

The Enemy's Love

Horseneck

I sit by this ocean
the waves crashing in
the shoreline keeps changing
this mood that I'm in,

and the waters receding
like the love that's inside
my heart keeps on bleeding
to know love has lied,

and the fever within me
is cooled by the wind
as the cold breeze that blows
confirms love has sinned,

To release all my passion
this ocean would burst
if it were compassion
could not quench my thirst.

The sun is now falling
the night it will steal
this fire inside me
that just cannot heal

this ripping desire
of love to explode
when morning arrives
so will love's hold.

as the waves keep on swelling
I sink in the sand
I can sit here forever
revenge is at hand
      this ocean will wail
      but love will command.

I sit by this ocean
the waves crashing in
the shoreline keeps changing
this mood that I'm in

and the waters receding
like the love that's inside
as my heart keeps on bleeding
to know love has died.

                                            For PM, 1976

Knowing You

Most my friends think
        I've gone mad
that I speak of you so free
that I love you is no secret
nor the fact you don't love me
        I see that as no concern
            though they think it ought to be.

people think I've
        been had
that I threw my love away
but they never spent a night
like the night you said I may
        or held you in their arms
            for which I'd give it all to stay

and the world knows
        that I'm sad
cause the frown is showing through
but somewhere deep inside
I would not change the view,
        or the fact,
            or the joy,
                or the thrill,
of knowing you.

A Daisy

If I should die
    restore me one hour
hand me a flower
    a daisy will do,
and I will have lived
    one gift
        one love
            one lifetime
    more than you.

Zooming Turtles Born Free

Those sleepy jejune days
rolling the grasses
counting the green limber blades
blowing the white starry lions
      after yellow they grew
      as I thought we knew
the world would be ours.

things were simple and plain
those that were not
of delusional concern,
for we were babes
our backs trusted to the
handlers of timely affairs—
      zooming eagles born free,

      those golden streets
      and silver walkways
      reflect better days
      when i was young
      running the flowered meadows
      by rushing streams
      forever screaming
      always beaming.

(and the giant's words)
      we've majestic wings you know
      and you will too
      when of age you'll see,

    you'll glide the heavens
    and soar the earth
for we are zooming turtles born free. yes ...

memory soothes me well
with surging visions
of dancing fancies
anted gutters
and lizard stones,
a world of stern smoking fathers
dutiful scrubbing mothers
spent in endless races
    in endless seasons
        among endless friends.

let us throw love and respect
to the hills and woodlands
to shine upon us again.
let us sing to the fresh arriving babes—
    we've majestic shells you know
    and you will too
    when of age you'll see,
    you'll lift your load
    gnash your teeth
    for we are zooming turtles
    born free.

those early spring years

      of squishy rubber balls
      of hard wooden bats
      games in brim hats,
when rules were hammers
in the winds of my father's mind,
remembering the rain
when clouds were just floating water
and blue was a colored sky
unlike the cracks in my brow
or the law to show
how we need not try.

come skip with me
count the seams in walkways
on empty school days
mold the fluffy animal skies
forget the coming winters
the future—
to dream
snooze in my yesterday mind
never to awake
to the fear they may rake.

Another Monday Morning (song)

It's another Monday morning
        the scarlet horizon secrets the sun
I'm recovering from a late night of mourning
        another day without has begun.

slip into a shirt
        thread on my jeans
                walk down the stairs
                        and out of the door
my heart is crazing, with fractured seams
I'll travel through the day and not get far.

there is no distance I can cover
        attractions or places I want to see
without passion one cannot be a lover
without you around I just can't be free.

it's another evening sunset
        dark skies welcome the migrating moon
lying in bed with my only regret
        you're not in my arms to lighten the gloom.

but I will recover and even survive
        another Monday, another year
keeping the passion and feelings alive
        the dreams and desire of having you here.

                                          For BK, 1989

Painting Dreams (song)

Promised to paint my life alone
        and dry it by the wind and sun
but—
along you came and stained the heart
        colors now have begun to run.

love is not my favorite tone
        heart never gets a chance to dry,
the canvas always soaked with tears
        to leave the tints and shades to die.

truth is what the light cry's out
        can't draw your image it seems,
you run from love I have to give
        I'm left alone just painting dreams.

painting dreams,
painting dreams,
        your portrait my mind can't erase
painting dreams,
painting dreams,
        never awakening to see your face.

had no fear of darkening skies
        spurn the thunder, guffaw at the wind,
did not need you when you yearned me
        dismissal appeared the way to win.

now grassy fields have all gone brown
        can't paint the flowers that turn from me,
distant hills conceal the sun
        the open landscape's just not free.

painting dreams,
painting dreams,
        the only way I get my sleep,
painting dreams,
painting dreams,
        pastels of you are all I keep
                tinting all the days
                it never pays
                        painting dreams.

November Search (song)

Cousin of April and birth
aging time of November frost,
wandering streets of toasted leaves
love bond heart with dreams a lost.

shoulders keep red ears warm
crisp blue sky smiles at the sun,
unknowing souls walk on by
feelings fixed with my past undone.

someone shoot the night with fire
the frozen moon stares down on me,
bitter air impale the bones
the inert light lacks sympathy.

cry—
cry hard with the cold morn rain
New England nights always hurt,
dig a hole
entomb warm times
deep in the ground
the sleepless earth.

run—
run, slowly through early winter snow
beware not to stumble on granite curbs,
a night with stars in hypnotic stare
best take the hint of Canadian birds.

unlike cousins of April and death
the living time, the November fight,
woolen armor protects against
a wandering soul in spiritual flight.

biting lips bite and burn
shuttered windows by barren sheets,
smoking chimneys and black horizons
winter stunts for all who sleeps.

crackling wood splits the silence
in intervals of weeping reminders,
ice storm rages and chases December
in your mind's squall you'll never find her.

rusty trees sieve blaring screams
and shiver with the razor wind,
always to return and paint the sky
and fight the snow that melts within.

Autumn of My Eye (song)

The years keep wheeling past
      I'm still not ready now
warmer days no longer last
      reaper now swallows the plow,

there's no stopping the coming frost
      I see your fading colors fly
time of year I'm always lost
      you the Autumn of my eyes,

funny how nature slowly turns
      lovers love, then move on
rain not always comes from clouds
      when Fall arrives you're always gone,

Winter will freeze, harden the heart
      save it for the long-off spring
when love returns for a new start
      the sun will soothe winter's sting,

when again I let my passion flow
        repeat the same fast mortal mistake
let my love for you pass go
        fail to ready for winter's take,

and once again I entomb the seed
        a woman's love that always dies
when it is cold, I'm left in need
        and you the autumn of my eye,

and the years keep wheeling past
        I'm still not ready now
falling leaves are dropping fast
        can't seem to learn somehow,

some lovers stay, still others go
        like Summer birth which sooner dies
you have become my Winter snow
        the Autumn of my eye.

The Struggle

The swelling silence outside
this bedroom window is pressure
to my ears and is muffled only by
the absolute absence of sound
in this empty unlit space.

       these tired cells which were once my brain
       make clear the essence of things
       that they are still the same
the heart still in a hemorrhaging state.

It's hard to get up with this massive weight
       that pins my hollow chest
       to these icy wanting sheets.

eyes— brown weeping binoculars
       left out in the cold night rain
       secreted the salty moisture
       that dehydrates the soul
as they struggle for vision of the
foreign shadows that refuse
to hold focus around me.

       the smell is one of emptiness
       the cold air infiltrates
       these swollen nostrils
       fanning tears that still settle
       deep in my throat.

but my mouth is dry,
dry as a wound stuffed with cotton and gauze,
my lips fractured
like a dusty desert floor ... never kissed
and an empty stomach growls
in a muffled battle with the
evening wine that saturates its walls
in fermented memories,
memories of you,
memories still burning
like a good whiskey gone stale
rancid in this empty glass of day.

only the dim dawn light
which filters through the wavy glass
and window that feeds this bedroom fortress
alerts me another day welcomes itself
rudely welcomes itself,
        entering without invitation.
and this vastness
        this wasteland to my left
                this desert
                      this barren ocean
                              this universe of space
reminds me of the indisputable fact
        that I must act—
                another day
        that I must attack—
                another night
        without you.

For BK, 1984

The Enemy's Love (song)

Been countless years
been a week
good times and laughter are precious few
this sacred sword has left me weak
the battle seems lost, and so do you.

    this crusade's a futile deception
    like the porous armor I continue to wear
    for the love I give receives no redemption
    despite my strength, it's all I can bear.

you see, I partake in a celibate war
a campaign of love is a messy art
the less you give, I battle for more
should have retreated right from the start.

    been countless years
    been a week
    good times and laughter are precious few
    this sacred sword has left me weak
    the battle seems lost and so do you.

I wheel this cutlass of ice, of fire
A bloody heart on my sleeve
I fight from my knees
but this steeplechase of love and desire
has lost its passion and hunger for these.

      inside I lose this weapon called pride
      the scares though aged continue to bleed
      to a solider of passion zeal will subside
      when the enemy's love becomes his need

for it's been countless years, its been a week
good times and laughter are precious and few
this sacred sword has left me weak
and the battle seems lost and so do you.

                                        For BK, 1982

Skunk's Tail

Dazzled by the diamonds on his roof
he gathered himself together
and the shimmering moon glow
of a warm summer's night
made his coat look better.

for it was time for his prowl
the late hour of the owl
that he would catch her
he would fetch her
his love.

so grooming he did
his tail, his paws
for cleanliness and nature
were his only laws
and out he went
piercing the night
smelling fine
with the moon as his light.

now, on a distant hill
on the other side
of the road did abode
Miss Bunny
his honey
his dove
scanning the air
for the scent of her love.
she stood on her hinds
aware of the times
like many before,

"he would never be late"
for he was a chap
of dignity and flair
and missing a date
to him was quite rare.

but ...

this day was like no other before
"an hour late," Bunny screamed by the door
               waiting,
                            stating,
"where could he be
he is never this late
an hour has past
does he know of our date?"

and indeed he did
for humble he was
and missing the date
was not of his cause.

for a highway you see
which he had to cross
was where Miss Bunny
had gained her loss.

and with the aroma of a miasmic moon
she hopped into bed
crying about her love
who lay in tar dead.

                                        1976

Brenda's Eyes (song)

She came to me in the dead of night
        and filled the barren sky with stars
made it shine and alive with light
        released the bonds and broke the bars.

I can't help but love her
        hidden passion now have no ties
since the night we first kissed
        I lost myself in Brenda's eyes.

cannot forget the way she looked
        the night we danced and held on tight
my love I gave—my heart she took
        in her arms I gave up the fight.

and like fiery tides that come and go
        Autumn colors that wither and die
need comfort from the wind and blow
        to warm my heart in Brenda's eyes.

but now she's gone I heard tell
        another shares her precious night
love was pinned right where I fell
        was it wrong if it felt so right.

and I can't help but love her
        hidden passion now strained with lies
that night we danced and held on tight
        and I lost myself in Brenda's eyes.

                                    For BK, 1989

Watching the Monkeys

My Stranger, My Lover

Sign reads "departure"
I file up the steep causeway
one stranger following the other
like ants on a march up a tree
up, up, up.

to the flight back home
the romantic Madeira sun
        soon to be a tepid memory.

across the airport's atrium
you amble down the stairway
Funchal ahead for you
its warmth, its passions, allure
like a tear of joy
trickling down a happy face
down, down, down.

across this vast space
our eyes embrace
tangled in intimate hover
my stranger, my lover
I can hardly believe it
could it really be
you, you, you.

I have felt you many a time
walking by my side
my star, twinkling
lying by me, never far
pillows piled one upon another
with little need
for a bed so broad
blankets so infinite
me for your quilt
you as my sheet
reflecting the night
sharing a heat.

but,
the wave of those following
a tide of legs, arms, bags
pushing, heaving, surging
carrying you away
forever if not today
to the heat of this island garden
where I soon lose sight of you
to this Portuguese sky
never to hold
leaving me cold
fortune to know
        my stranger, my lover

mate to my soul,
paths lost perchance
future amiss
by the length of an airport foyer.
misaligned in time
and never to be mine
with faith expired
you are lost,
        forever,
and though we never have met
you were never found
you are my stranger, my lover.

I End My Day

I end the day bent
washing my face over
this basin of tepid water—
draining,
thinking now,
thinking how,
the staining I remove.

I pull the plug
letting the water go down
letting us down
leaving only two
damp, barren vessels
a porcelain heart
a shattered ego
and you
dry and indifferent.

Cardoza

Your reflection was blinding
leaving the slate of my mind
clean and yearning.

following months of song
I wooed you—you said yes

I met you at your home
your father was perched
in a fat tweed chair
swayed like a dry mumbling reed
bottles sprouting
        on the floor around him.
his upper lip curled and quivering.

he slurred "she is spoken for, you know"
and reprimanded my attempt
to win your love.

you laughed at the things he said
I chuckled at what you fed
      "Daddy likes his drink"
          you shed

six months afterward you were wed.
now, I spend long nights sitting
swaying like a reed
to the treachery in the deed

as my eyes came into focus
I laughed at the bottles
that sprout out from
the floor around me while
my upper lip curled and quivered.

Blind Date

There is no date that is blind,
to he given the gift
of foresight and vision
to recognize the value in another
and to extract the treasures
which reflect like a mirror
the value within ourselves.

there is no date that is blind
to she who can draw on the profits
which are offered at no cost
by he who receives and appreciates
the gift of friendship
which is given freely.

there is no date that is blind
when compared to a lifetime
when compared to a year
when compared to a week
when compared to a few short hours
which two strangers may share.

for it matters not how diverse
we may be
how refined our desire
be it for love or fire.

we are identical
in that we search for the same end
a relief to the loneliness
an illusive search for companionship
which may be totally
different in color

but—
illuminated by the same light
shared in the same night
and splintered in time.

Twelve Over Twelve

The first dozen
      conveys I'm sorry
the second to
      proclaim you're fine,
it I pushed beyond
      the boundaries
if I stepped
      across the line
when I ran
      instead of walking
when my words
      all seemed benign
must let my heart
      do all the talking
if I plan
      to make you mine.

For Deborah, someone who gave love with the properties of water, transparent, insipid, and as lasting as a bird bath in a tropical drought. I was surprised that the flowers lasted as long as they did.

Ardith in the Rain

We left the art museum
the Boston sky began to gray
you ran down to the Charles
I gave chase without delay

we were two Americans in Paris
of all the wonders I have seen
from Whistler onto Sargent
and to Cassatt and in between

it was you I came to see
to admire and adore
as the sky gave up its tears
and a torrent began to pour

still there's nowhere I want to be
or treasures I may obtain
then to spend a day with Ardith
running in the rain.

Sell Me ... Adore

I am forgetting
forgotten
what it all is about
how you took your love
from within, to without

tell me
lend me
sell me ... adore
      like a wounded lion
      I breach and I roar

that the sweetness
you barter
is my purpose to live
hearts that you culled
can I ever forgive

with candied kisses
baked with stale lust
embrace which you offer
I assume with mistrust

I am for forgetting
forgotten,
what it's like to survive
must I purchase your love
to keep me alive
wet fused ardor
I must beg to procure
as a shameful martyr
this charm I un'dure

tell me
lend me
sell me ... adore
       a malignant lover
         pleading for more
and if you should take back
this love you mentor
leave me not barren
       sell me ... adore

By Bread ... Alone

To this hunger be humble
though it may be true
man cannot subsist
by bread alone,
cannot subsist
without you ... alone
without you.

Down the Aisles of Oak Grove

Down the aisles of Oak Grove
    we take photos of trees
by finely cut stone
    where our spirits run free
you and I all alone
    as I crave it to be.

and strolling ahead
    you follow the path
as I chase from behind
    we hike and we chat
like a puppy in need
    or chasing a cat.

and with finger you push
    with lens you draw in
commanding the shutter
    and my soul from within
little do you know
    it's my head that you spin
my heart wanting you
    and my love you will win.

and as one by one
    pass the pillars of stone
you have little idea
    love for you has grown
down the aisles of Oak Grove
    I'll make you my own.

Watching the Monkeys

It was a crispy October
a day at the zoo
you were watching the monkeys
I was watching you

        you giggle,
        you laugh
        at the morsels of bread
        from your hand
        they snatch
        you clap every time
        the morsels they catch

I'm so fond of the little girl inside you
but it's the woman
I need
to follow
to lead

you walk by the lions
without even a glance
the cold bars contain them,
sometimes you walk by me in the same way
and I can't feel your love
fracture the extrinsic bars you display

the Adelies wobble
this way
        that way
        again, this way
orchestrated confusion on a comical stage
I seem to feel what they feel
wishing I knew what it was
this pleasure you steal

I rush up ahead to my second favorite attraction
the gallant polar bears
who show no reaction
to the admission that you are my first
        my first without infraction

        They stand nine feet high
        scratching the clouds in the sky
        such pride, such confidence
        I wish I felt about ... you

then...
You embrace me from behind
and rest your warm cheek upon mine
        "they're almost as tall as you"
you compliment in jest
        "I love it here" you say,
        "and I love you" I convey,

you smile and casually run away
a cold breeze cuts at the heart
the bears laugh in a growl
        "wait for me" I call out

you continue to the cage
the one with the owl
on a crispy day in October
a day at the zoo
you were watching the monkeys
and I was watching you.

                                          For BK

I Be Your Butter Your Jam

I be your butter your jam
to spread as you see fit
upon your jelly wishes
which craving from within
        deep yeast of desire
        to be smeared over dry lips
        with honey dripping fingers
        in obscene wet sweetness
in firm heated convulsion
only practiced by tangled lovers
between naked sheets of night
in moist unleavened embrace
cohesion upon which to feed
        I be your butter your jam.

Thru the Mall

We took a stroll thru the mall
        and I let you walk ahead,
                pretending to lace my shoe
                        so I could embrace you
from afar
with my eyes
embrace you in full view.

did not dare take long
instead, I ran up and clutched your hand
for you belong to me
        and I to you,
the mall must understand.

I stitch my fingers around yours
        and pull you tight
looking up you smile
all the while
knowing the blind date we had
has taken on sight.

I stroke your face
like braille it said ... "I'm happy"

gently you pucker and mail a kiss
and with a firm grip
place your arm around my waist
and tuck me in
      like a favorite flannel shirt
      to keep you warm from the storm
      of shoppers around us.

           (how lucky your clothing to
           be so close against you)

shoppers march by us
with unconcerned stares,
the men in painful resentfulness
they stumble with jealousy
because you belong to me,
the women with fingers crossed
behind their backs
wishing, wishing to have what we feel
all of them, wanting,
      wanting to steal
      this passion we have for each other.
a flock of teens fly by in dance
      children skip past and chant
           lyrical proclamations of freedom

but you are the only dance I need
my heart feels like a child around you
    skipping beat in lyrical affirmation
    that freedom means to be captive by you.
then suddenly you discover a clothing boutique
with a dress you find unique
and run up ahead
and leave me behind
pretending to lace my shoe
    so I could embrace,
    from a distance embrace,
    from one knee—
        embrace you in total view.

Need Ask God, What For

From the beginning of time
God created the lion
with strength and a majestic mane
>   to wander the jungle
>   and lie in the fields
>   to rule, to slay and to rein

at the commencement of time
God created the impala
to leap in the sky
and touch the sun
>   speed that could blind
>   with grace and with poise
>   swiftness he could gather and run

from the foundation of time
in God's surreptitious design
the lion raises high his paw
>   and from limb to limb
>   he shreds and tears
>   till there is an impala no more
>>   in my mind
>>   in my heart
>>   need ask God
>>   ... what for?

Your Weakness Does Mar

Your weakness does mar
sins injected by parental harm
you are left with a twisted rudder
jammed, jammed
circling life in selfish turmoil
harvesting those entrapped in your wake

a mind blistered
a heart snared
by the blunt rusted barbs beneath
the beauty behind an angelic reflection

in a pool crystal black as ink
where I drown in mire
and weakness
a weakness that mars
in apathy and fragile esteem
of my own

your weakness does mar
my soul tangles in this infected
desire of untruth and adulterated
passion for an illusion
a mermaid's song sucking
to your rock
using the weakness
that is your strength
an infirmity, an epitaph
in failed attempt to swell
emasculated endeavor to fill with love
from an empty basin drained

passion pours wasted
for your porcupine gift
punctures affection
leaving a soul
filled with sand
to choke
to bake
in fermented weed
no flower
no seed.

Sacred Anvil

I endure this loneliness
a sacred anvil strung low
tethered firmly about the neck
it strangles ... giving no reprieve

instead I trip over this iron
and fall at your feet
in shameful begging

I am conservator to you in your free time
a puppet
crumbling crust for your cream pie of life
never feeling more alone than when you are with me,
aching more than when you are away and not sitting on
this anvil, pecking my cheek with tarnished lips of betrayal,
kisses that would cause Judas to drop his silver in blush,
with embraces tight as a tiny crab
pinching my desire for comfort
a tease, a hook lacking line
where I continue to cast my net
into a barren sea.

I fan this self-imposed loneliness
like a bellows
inflicted like a lonely blacksmith
in need of hammer and flame
to temper your requests,
to harden the resolve,
to sever the chain
that snarls my heart to this mass of sacred steel
which you employ as your sacrificial
alter for your hollow offerings of love,
weighing down my heart with craving
always with craving for more.

Friendship Passes Away

Your desire is that we be friends
just as we once never were.

You claim your shallow wounds have healed
paper cuts to your heart long faded
and the moment has arrived for forbearing
to band-aid the sting of blame
to mend emendable guilt

your prickly kiss stings my cheek
like my mother's fiberglass curtains
one arm embraces
like a hunched Notre Dame bell ringer
a butterfly leech lacking open arms.

you say you are pleased I moved on,
though I still stand in the same
place you left me—if you would only notice.

you laugh and say I look good.

you add I would worship your new beau
how similar we both are
a mirror smiling,
how you are looking forward to our
new campaign of friendship.

    little do you realize
    I expired from my injury
your banished apathy,
    the stitches never held

    in love gone gangrenous
    friendship passes away
shortly after.

Where I Can Never Go

Like a wandering moon
in pursuit of a retreating sun
you and I will never rise together.

in the dark side of your world
on the burning surface of my passion
we can only eclipse one another
for the light you shed
is not yours to give
and warmth reflected
only to the laughing stars
in twinkling chuckles, lost
in space and in time.

I can only have you singed
and with your altering faces
wandering the heavens
will only leave me with
pucks, barren and cold
clinging to the dark side
of your heart
the undiscovered country
where no love burns
a place where even you
have not gone
where I can never go
or wish to be.

THE DARKNESS

Poetry Is

One need not know the anatomy of a flower
                to write about its beauty
nor does one need to be a trained surgeon
                to reach the heart

one need not be a schooled medical man
                to access the mind
or be a master engineer to study love

neither does one need to know God
                to marvel at the universe

such is poetry
        a thing beautiful as a flower
warm as a heart
        vast as a mind
passionate as love
        almost
as never-ending
as God.

Waiting

On a still, quiet afternoon
I wander the sterile grounds
of carefully placed stones
of red, of white marble
of polished granite grey
unappreciated by those who lie
covered, silent endlessly
waiting
waiting
waiting away

the hemorrhaging foliage
on bleeding trees
tumble to the ground at my feet
on a bed of late summer grass
where they will not long last
dry and wither
crumble and decay
steady and unnoticed
from beneath this clay

like the flesh we carry
until the day we marry
the lying leaves
those below
waiting
waiting
waiting away.

Ice House at Interlachen

Ice castle partitions
      speak by a placid shore
with no king to deliver
      growing trees at its core
   now dry and parched
holding ice no more

by a New England loch
      this land by the lake
of speckled glass granite
      in the sun left to bake
   now nothing to give
and nothing to take

outside this woodland
      a world paved ground
denizens of ignorance
      where no essence is found
   history dies
in this once ancient town

thus Bohemian fathers
      with frozen block minds
by acuity which melts
      the ages behind
   of the small and the blind
      to those left to time
having no reverence for quest
           or vision of kind.

Borden Utopia Gone

Skeleton rock footing
held hostage in shade
not by the saplings
and trees which evade
      with poured rasped mortar
           cartilage between stone
      now crumbling in moss
the soul left alone

rock heap upon rock
forsake where it lay
unlike generations
inclined not to stay
      in a dawdle spring moon
           admiring ponies at night
      till his cane felt the loss
a ghost gone to light

windswept fields now jungles
where children had run
his progeny played
with dogs in the sun
      now conquered by maple
           the locust, the pine
      did it pass in place
or existed once in time

the only tribute
is this wiry crag wall
skeleton rock footing
where a house once tall
lie now in ruin
on the ground where it fall.

Upon discovery of Interlachen at Fall River, Massachusetts, and the former home of Spencer Borden

Upon Filming Interlachen

You wane well behind
your feet plowing leaves
brown bone flaky nature
as we will once all be
moist peat, windswept decay
that clings to your heels
you filming away

you saunter along slowly
a camera for one eye
a cyclopic adventure
treasures unearth or found
keeping record of your world
the sights— the sound

with my back to the path ahead
I let my toes lead the way
making certain
you still follow
making certain
you will stay

you walk alone
while I stumble amongst the trees,
we all follow in
      your little magical humming box
      images captured inside
for you to delight later
      the me you arrest
for you to enjoy
even long after the camera
is long put away
and the humming has stopped
at the end of the day.

The Pawn

There be the pawn
to slay and kill
on foreign soil
        an invading guest
        for honor and glory
        he will die for oil

on a game board of lies
of politics and prayer
for God and country,
        where the soul is pillaged
        and carnage will flood
        with remittance in flesh
                he's anointed in blood

there be the pawn

this youth who fight
but perceptions so light
with no king to guide
or a leader in sight

and the political elite
        whose daughter and son
are deferred from the heat
        in a distant lost land
from death in the street

a puppet in war
not a play for the rich
where no money can cure
a wound you can't stitch
       where moral decay
       be the Republican's itch

there be the pawn

into battle he'll stun
a youth in his dawn
a warrior undone
on a political whim
at the point of a gun
in cause without merit
a battle is won.

The Darkness

I set out for home
and the darkness follows
as my long winter shadow
darts ahead
like a flat crushed companion
all the time knowing
the darkness will
fade, absorb him in silence
a blanket of nothingness

the sun scurried with fright
to a distant and remote,
horizon fractured by the city
perched on the hill jagged
like children's building
blocks heaped one on another
their orange windows
kissed by the sinking sun, blazing
church steeples like abandoned needles
poking the clouds
empty of rain and forgiveness
in search of God

the moon emerges from behind me
in silent ambush to smolder with
light to which it can make no claim
just a plucked ornament dangling
in a sad umbra to illuminate
the uncertainties that eat inside

and so, I quicken my pace
in my own desperate haste
to beat the darkness
from white to red to grey
the gloom about to fall
to black.

Void in the Earth

A naked foundation of fieldstone and granite
once vision of a soul long plucked away
over stone horseshoe eyebrows
        along honed crescent wall
                vista to meadow and pond
of panoramas beyond
now woefully dismissed
        abandon,
        gone

just an abyss for the green
growing haughty and high
from an open wound grave
dug by those who lay
in chasms dug by those
themselves all lost from memory
like the master once here
        with all left just a mere, empty void
        in earth

standing along
these deprived basement walls
I envision exotic fine wood
supple silk, lace,
      wavy stained glass panes
           sturdy, dignified partitions
on this natty stacked stone
with all that is left

broken twigs and dry leaves
snap under new feet
in sad Victorian defeat
its all that is left
to the big house beneath.

Upon the discovery of Interlachen and the foundation of the old home of Spencer Borden, breeder of Arabian horses in Victorian Fall River, Massachusetts.

Depression Train

I sit on this lumpy stuffed chair
Jethro Tull thunders in the room
reverberating loudly, progressive, lyrical.

      my head resting back
      eyes on a watery fuzzy ceiling
      waiting for this empty black train
      to pass.

Tull is my syringe
my hypodermic release,
      the music sutures
      without producing a scar
      it leaves me "Thick as a Brick."

tears burn down my face
hanging— tickling my nose
      not inducing laughter
      they flood and bathe dry lips
      continue down to hide in my beard
      to settle, cling to my damp hidden chin.

my fingers tire and ache
clutching the soiled arms of this chair
      a hundred phlebotomists stick me
      with blunt obtuse needles
though I feel no corporal pangs
and no blood is drawn,
      I am alone and it is good.

as this silent illusive dark train
roars on through
my ambitions, my dreams, shudder fervently
these grey spongy rails vibrate violently in my head
but I know my cerebral tracks are sturdy
my reasoning treads and spikes robust
tomorrow will be another day
and the train will be distant
        it always is,
                always has,
                        always will,

I will not be shaken
hush will be restored once more
and I will be able
once again, instead—
to listen to love songs and smile.

To Australia

I once granted a great
sum of money to a
pastor.

I reasoned it was what
God required of me.

he was going home
to Australia to accept
a high paying job.

read in the paper
that an executive embezzled
a great sum of money.

he thought it was what
God wanted him to do.

perhaps he will go
to Australia and
become a pastor.

Met A Man

I was searching for truth
When I met a man who informed me
There was no God,
    I knew I had met a fool.
    And quickly moved away.

I was probing and longing
And met a man who notified me
He was intimate with God,
    I thought him reckless
    From him I broke away.

I needed tranquility
And met a man who declared
He spoke to God,
    I knew he was confused
    I left him to converse alone.

I felt lost and lonely
And met a man who insisted
God spoke to him,
    I knew he was dangerous
    From him I made my escape.

I was digging for inspiration
When I met a man
Who was searching for God,
    We walked in peace a while,
    Spoke of ignorance and profound wisdom.

You are Aging Gracefully

You listed your three
most desires:
eating,
making love,
and a long satisfying
visit to the toilet.

now that the years
have passed you by
a long satisfying
visit to the toilet
has tossed making love
out of second place.

nice to know
you are aging
gracefully.

Rainbow Clown

Take fear
      the Rainbow Clown
with a frozen smile,
somehow funny
somewhat vile.

take watch
      the black dressed priest
with a ledger from God,
he digs your grave
with a grin and nod.

peel back your eyes
      to the statesman's fist
legislator's son,
with the stroke of a pen
loads, triggers the gun.

use heed with
      the pure lover's mien
a touch and a tear,
a stony heart
is what you should fear.

take fear
the Rainbow Clown.

Animals, Animals

Animals, animals
love people

        people, people
        love animals

animals and people
eat animals

        people eat and
        love animals

people love
people and
love animals,

        eat people

animals and
people eat and
love people,

        eat animals

love animals
animals, animals.

I would like to thank my publisher for her extensive efforts in assembling this book and to Patricia Stafford for a job well done.

The front cover of *The Sadness I Take to Sea and Other Poems* is a photograph taken just southwest of Martha's Vineyard at N41 13 69 and W71 00 56, at the break of day, from the s/v Saudades, late spring 2010, after a thirteen day offshore passage from Florida to New England. An attempt for the shutter to capture the tiny island of Noman's Land, just south of the Vineyard, was in vain do to the lack of light and the early morning mist and fog which scattered the light. Instead, what was captured was this colorful poetic image.

www.ingramcontent.com/pod-product-compliance
Lightning Source LLC
Chambersburg PA
CBHW051651040426
42446CB00009B/1088